89%

SARAH COOPER

CLEMSON
LITERATURE SERIES
CONVERSE

As a partnership between Clemson University Press and the Converse College Low Residency MFA program, this series publishes poetry collections, short-story collections, and creative nonfiction.

89%

SARAH COOPER

CLEMSON
UNIVERSITY
PRESS

Cover design by Lindsay Scott
Typeset in Minion Pro by Jae Dyche
Cover image by Megan Llewellyn

For information about Clemson University Press,
please visit our website at www.clemson.edu/press.

for Mom, who showed me what love can do.

for Lesley, let's do it, all of it.

CONTENTS

BACKGROUND RESEARCH

I was born to have you and you were born to listen to my advice.

Family Education

Your great-grandfather killed himself, she says. My salad fork chinks against plate, falls beside kalamata olive, stops adjacent to cherry tomato. I hold her eyes in our mother-daughter stare.

He sat in his evening chair, the one with a worn headrest from his sweaty scalp. He always smoked in that chair, puffing cigarettes he rolled tightly after dinner. One night he slipped into sleep, dreamed too hard, never felt the cigarette leave his finger, fall on the stack of newspapers. He never woke from that sleep.

Smeared eyeliner lingers on lashes that keep posing as floodgates. Still we hold this gaze. She whispers, *these are the kind of memories you have to keep, hold them like a family handkerchief, fold along the lines, build a square; something you can do without looking, making it your own.*

My Love Asks When I Began Writing Poems

"…for I often part with things I fancy I have loved, - sometimes to the grave, and sometimes to an oblivion rather bitterer than death…" – Emily Dickinson, 22, Early Middle Writings, Mid – 1850s to mid-1860s

I was twelve. It read, "I love Katie D.,
        her hair falls like willow branches over freckled shoulders."
                These poems were exits from my body. No one taught me

how to pass, how correct myself, how to straighten.
        I learned to keep a straight face, you think it's my game face
                but Love, I want to tell you: *it is the face that kept me from showing*

everyone all the wanting my mouth hungered for.
            By sixteen my bitten cheeks were
                    scar tissue canvases hanging

from a mouth chewed quiet. My molars finally learned
        how to hold skin without biting, without clenching,
            without beckoning the blood to trickle down throat.

In my treehouse I burned those poems:
        let flicker grow to flame, watched edges curl to black,
            read words in reverse until fire met eyeline.

My Love, all those poems are ashes
        below two trees that once suspended me.
            I buried those traces or on windy days offered them a breezy escape.

My stoic face was no contender for words
        about loving girls, about wanting to love girls.
            Love, I have burned and buried my youth.

When my life is over, honor
        those poems and those girls.
            Promise you'll cremate me.

DRAFTING

I always let her
win; draft her stride, smell

Herbal Essences in her hair,
Tide in her t-shirt. Heat-stricken

feet from pavement kick and arms
pump our strides up a double-hilled

mountain driveway. In dreams
I imagine my hand reaching

for her body, stopping the run,
spin her toward me. What would I say?

What did I know to do
at eight years old? I had seen

my parents embrace: coffee mugs dangling
from the hand not wrapped

in a morning hug.
Do you drink coffee? I finally ask.

That stuff tastes terrible!
I nod, *Yeah, me either.* Feeling her

look at me I motion for the run to commence.
I want to follow her.

Remember where you came from because it's where I will always
be with a warm fire, my knitting needles,
an open ear and a bottle of Patron®.

I GET BY WITH A LITTLE HELP FROM MY FRIENDS,

she says. Because "menopause" sounds medical and worse: inescapable. Her menopause has become everyone's reality: the cats scramble for rattling of pilled estrogen in bottles, her new proclivity of belting out The Beatles' while trying to remember why she opened the pantry in the first place is routine. I pull into the driveway one night to see her standing in Victoria's Secret Underwear, barefoot, flowing blouse pulled over her head, arms stretched above, pants lost somewhere indoors because now she is outside: dancing. Dim the headlights to watch her Game Over hips jive to a song she's singing, see her twirl across the porch, avoiding the Adirondack chairs, and dog who naps unscathed. She's two-stepping, clogging, maybe waltzing and I am witnessing the serenity of change, and a hot flash. She wraps her arms around me, *Dinner is free, but the show will cost you $20.*

I'm always proud of you. So, remember that when you think about making a mockery of my words.

Make Straight Lines

If you vertical the blade, you won't cut yourself.
Keep your hand steady. Make sure you have plenty

of soap, lather your legs, don't shave past the knee,
she instructed. But knees

and upper leg were tangles of hair, arms overgrown,
eyebrows intertwined (where no hair should be).

I shaved between them for months
before anyone knew. Mom recognized the dry skin,

the uneven lines. After school I sat in a salon,
shreds of paper pressed around my eyebrows;

"shaping" this was called. Hot
wax smelled like melting skin, red and puffy, smooth.

I lay with a girl: hips sweat slick,
fingers probe through hair, carefully,

around, between, exploring. Years later I straddle
a woman who shaves: everything.

This is what being queer is, I thought,
erase, make smooth your body: I stood in the dorm bathroom

staring into the full-length mirror, I cut away
as much as I could, shaved my inner thighs

until finally my lips stared back.
I watched as the pubic hairs and Dove soap suds

dripped from the razor, ran my fingertips
over skin freshly found.

My lips no longer hidden by a thicket.
I made myself exposed.

THURSDAY NIGHT AT THE ISLANDER

When a man at the bar says to you, *Maybe you should date a guy, you might like it!* you fire back, *Maybe you should date a guy, you might like it.* Of course, he feels this to be an absurd idea. You feel vindicated by your suggestion but silently embarrassed you must vindicate anything at all. Still, you low-five yourself under the lip of the bar, turning the proverbial table on bigotry that masquerades as a pickup line. Maybe some small town will hear of this, ask you to come give a speech, give you a key to the city and maybe a ride in the Christmas parade, "Our Fearless Lesbian Leader." But for now, you are proud, queer proud. Then you think of all the other social problems that could almost be solved this way: the wage gap, un-neutered cats, seven-minute ab videos and twerking. You realize the true issue: We need to counter problems not with solutions but perspective. You apply this principle with the man who has become your bar project. *It's a shame your body will go to waste,* he announces, smirking. The boil of your blood is not what he should fear, nor the speed of your right hook. You want to tell him that only pathetic women fall for that logic, weak women, women who desperately want to swim within the lanes of heteronormativity, women who yearn to perform femininity without hesitation. But you don't. Calmly, you speak. *You only want me because you know you cannot have me. I am the Mount Everest of women, a grand view from afar, yet when close insurmountable. This type of body requires special training to conquer. It was built to waste the bravest men.*

If you're cooking without wine, you're wasting your time.

PINOT GRIGIO

Always I am always thirsty and needing to have more. This is more than true. If you get on your knees in the grocery you can find the biggest and cheapest bottle of pinot grigio on the bottom shelf. It will be dusty and dazed but it's drinkable, you know? And I am a feaster of wine, as you know. I sample whites from California and New Zealand, sucking my tongue into a V, let the droplets seep into the buds of my tastes. I sip from stemless glasses, let lips linger around rims only to remember this mouth has appraised its apple finish, its pear beginning before. Tasting is the antithesis of you: never have I seen you as a washed wine glass, a goblet repurposed. I cup you inside my hands, fingers interlocked let you slosh freely, never spilling. On rainy days my ambitious self wants to sketch a map, show you spaces that are me (land) and the projected me (water). But you would see the lakes and streams pouring through and question if I am drowning in possibilities. (I'm not.) I breaststroke these waters as a test: the potential of drowning is scary because really anything can happen and I've never been too sure about leg cramps or what lurks in the great lakes but with you I can float (eyes closed, supine). I'm intelligently captivated with you, rippled into the current of your sea kelp eyes. I thirst for you. It began as an evening like all the rest with me writing and the candles flickering against my stemmed wine glass, three sips left, final inspiration or a generous numbing to stanzas. I read. I swallow. I reach for you.

You are too strong to be told who you are so don't listen to anyone, but me,
because I'm not just anyone.

A Conversation with my Mother

Why do you call yourselves lesbians?

> *Well, Mom, the poet,*
> *Sappho,*
> *had an all-girls school.*

Like Sweet Briar?

> *Sure, like Sweet Briar*
> *anyways, this school was*
> *on the Isle of Lesbos. She fell*
> *in love with one of her students,*
> *Anaktoria. That's presumably*
> *where lesbian is derived.*

Oh, I see, well, it sounds rather
diagnostic but thanks for explaining.

One more thing: wasn't Sappho just a cougar?

You can love anyone, just don't stay with the wrong one.

Performing Basic Instinct

Our eyes peer across
      library books shelved
           and staggered against encyclopedia volumes.

We brush knuckles
      in lunch lines, fingers collide
           to pluck plastic forks and napkins.

Finally knee bumps under desks
      not to signal the other
           to read a passage aloud.

Years before I'd bleed:
      blotch white underwear in biology lab,
           I would feel her hand muffle my gasps.

Between sleeping bag zippers
      we gripped one another's wrists, hovered,
           pressed pubic bones together, squeezed.

I never told anyone. Did you?
      We were doing preparatory work,
           right? Practicing, yes?

We knew better
      than to seek refuge
           in sheets warm from daylight.

We knew better
      than to touch gently the body
           that resembled our own.

Everything is temporary except red wine stains and stretch marks.

My Mother as Lymph Nodes & Liver Lesions

As the doctor exits the exam room she reaches for my hand. I pull her entire body onto my lap as she stares at the Gastrointestinal Diagram like it's a map of the stars, searching for constellations, seeing only organs, glands, tissues. She whispers, *Do I need my liver to live?* I stare at her, feel her pelvic bones press into my thighs, her hands interlocking around my shoulders like she's a child asking if she has to get the flu shot. *Let's try to keep it,* I offer. I smell the loose skin on the back of her neck, watch a vein pulse, trace a map: clavicle to lymph node.

HYPOTHESIS & DATA

I gave birth to you, hours of physical pain with nothing to medicate me,
not even an Aleve, so remember: pain is always relative.

How things break

is by arguing
against options.
This horizontal structure
of past:
white stagnant against white;
white against gray-black words.
The air of loss
closes under oneself
with them;
the air of science.
The "how" things break
is by knowing expectations
deplete or decrease
or give
privilege too.
How things break
is for transcendent fear
obscure & non-able
to write oneself.
Fire, from flame,
complacent & still objects
danced upon:
log & kindling.
I shudder at your melting:
chunks clamoring, ice pick
cracking cubes
& snowplow gouging.
Your slight hands,
the left resting to the dusk
of my face, fleeting
on the water.
The way things break
is that always nothing attaches.

Hiking With an Erasure Heart
after Adrienne Rich's "The Floating Poem, Unnumbered" & years of Emily Dickinson & Sappho

plant some hydrangeas

        no-exchange rate currency

If hope   buy leashes

            things with feathers fly away?

 be fair [

                        ] earthy things

           wet dirt on boots   calloused hands

     handle, remember: thicketed bones of your torso [

                  ] blood pump is

        cylindrical symphonies

        evacuation

serenade space   one's partner

      somewhere else, some colder town

                     devour

contours of my pain.

Never eavesdrop unless you have a valid reason like curiosity.

DREAMING OF THE DEAD

Her lips parched, dry as pencil shavings,
curled, tinted where paint meets wood

where lips meet skin. She mouths
something, her body twitches

into white knuckled tension
sliding over metatarsals: they hold the dream.

I pry her fingers apart, hear:
I want my mom.

Tugaloo River

Veins stream toward lake
like a body creaks with fluid,

traverses sinew and tissue:
landscapes to meet the heart.

Last summer I camped your beds
and kayaked you, found a bridge,

its rotting pillars
splitting, boards grasping

one another to remain intact.
I thought of ways to save my mother

or ignore the disease, the cancer
that paddled her streams:

tumor growing, cells dividing,
the tumor her veins can't drown.

Damn the veins
that feed it. Let's paddle

her into a new river, off
the map, somewhere else.

There is a stain

on my Patagonia jacket: Christmas night
we huddled around welcoming chiminea,

drank rye whiskey, smoked Marlboros,
you turned too quickly, smeared cigarette ash through

my sleeve, took your lips near the burn,
blew, held my hand. I felt guitar string indentions

on your fingertips. You palmed the blisters
of my oarswoman hands. Our eyes

never met. Two years later
we sit on your porch, share a bottle

of Malbec. You play a song you wrote
a few years ago you say. I want to know

why you couldn't look at me that night.
Why now do you sing a song I can't hum?

I smell pine campfire,
hear embers spitting.

If you have a cat you will always have standards.

INSATIABLE

Mom eats salad every day for thirty years. Mom gets colon cancer. I buy her a juicer. Watch her drink water cast with vegetable pulp to appease me. I take to mashing her food: cauliflower, carrots, turnips, parsnips. I watch her salivate at Ruby Tuesday's commercial: a salad bar chockfull of broccoli florets, whole, like her hunger.

MORNING PRAYER

My mouth is a prison cell stocked with petrified word inmates.
Reassurance is the need to second-guess every nuanced mannerism.
I know she is only what I make her: sometimes I smile
when I can't understand, other moments I cry appreciation
and this moment I am speaking from mouth corners
she feels aimed toward her.

In another life I'll save lives instead of braiding words
because this life has left me speechless
and I'd rather diagnose heart failure than quote Dickinson

on the fly. Let me also say I've never wanted to live outside abundance
which looks like Glacier National Park, melting, making mud-puddled
streams: I retired my goulashes, sold my hiking poles
to wake against sun-crisp southern mornings.

I swear I don't love her:
I just want to be the cave her heart beats against
and send her the echoes like smoke rings when she leaves.

When my grandmother died her daughters
pried her mouth open to situate dentures.
This is what loyalty looks like, this is not about pride.

Hope is held in my ribcage:
it tries to seep through intercostal issue, escape the
naivety of my heart pounding symphonies, off-key.

For my thirteenth birthday I buried all my presents
in the backyard as time capsules. In school we
were taught to memorialize our presents
so later others could learn our practices.
I shudder at corrupting soil for ethnocentric ideologies.

Twenty years later I have no recollection
of what's buried. I promise I don't believe in permanence,
I say, *write your name across my chest and spell it "home."*

NINE PILLOWS

1. My mother has been
   deep breathing her entire life.
   It isn't trendy, like yoga, but
   it's useful like pigeon pose.

2. When I lie beside her, I put
   my arm between neck and pillow,
   wrap waist with the other, my nose
   burrowed in her shoulder.

3. She is every book
   I've never read.

4. I started syncing my breath
   with hers. As if the timeliness
   of inhale, exhale would keep
   us here, in a world that is
   eating her.

5. She can't count them, she feels the pressure they take from her hips,
   cushioning her bones.

6. Sometimes I place my head in her hands
   she glides her nails
   across my scalp, slowly.

7. I feel selfish
   for craving gestures, for needing
   anything from someone
   whose colon tumor was removed,
   osteotomy reversed, liver reduced
   to 25% and gallbladder extracted
   (it was in the surgeon's way).

8. I try to be present: ignore
   beeping machines, lights
   of monitors, the omniscient
   magnitude of living in a hospital.

9. This is what naps have become:
   a dance in dying, a chance
   to slip through pain, return for coffee.

A good friend will pull you through any situation. Well, maybe not you, you're so tall, but you're flexible and that will always come in handy.

COPING & OTHER TACTICS

I resort to
protein shakes
and eventually
pinot noir.
You made a joke
once that you *noir*
my native name
(as if I were native
of anywhere).
You said it gagging on a feeding tube.
Your inability to eat was replaced with a reflex not to swallow.
Eventually, you yanked
the tube,
an esophagus extraction,
wrapped it on the bed rail,
slept four hours,
the longest you'd slept in weeks.
When the nurse
tried to reinsert the line
you reached for the food tray,
choked down two slices of toast.

I Wanna be a Drag Queen

My calves, lean like tenderloin
       will stand in salute above stilettos. My eyes
       fiercely painted in thirteen shades of blue will lure

the audience into my performance – lips
       will part, pucker to "I'm Coming Out."
       My mouse-filled hair curled, teased

and shining must cascade
       down freshly shaven arms
       because when I grow up I will be a drag queen.

You would decorate
       me with sequins, ribbons, hair bands
       and strapless dresses.

I wanted to be just like you, wanted to walk
       on stage and feel the lights bounce
       across my sculpted thighs.

You would applaud my eyelashes glued on,
       double-curled, mascara-capped. All will cheer
       for my hips, structured like books on shelves, curving

as I swerve and sway, lips pursed, syncing.
       I want to bend, stand like you, fold my arms
       under my breast line and sass the audience;

              a presentress of gender, a bender of binaries, a queen.

Don't do anything to your body that gravity will impact.

Fireplace

Your clavicle v's toward throat's concave insert,
breasts still taught, nipples brown, shoulders sturdy,

veins sprawling toward chin,
a scar holding your torso together.

You rub lotion over your forehead, eyes, cheekbones
 now glisten, Lubriderm smeared over elbows.

Fastening bra with one hand, you talk to me,
stand in front of the fireplace, chattering about Dad:

his doctor's appointments, the referral to a specialist,
diagnosis sciatica. You want him to be well

(and for a moment we both forget you are not.)
Mom, you look good, I announce with a wink. I haven't seen

your body unclothed in over a year when we were living
in a hospital room together. I'd change your sheets,

your gown, we brushed our teeth at a sink,
you wanted to stand for that. It was out of dignity.

It was out of fear you could no longer stand,
it was out of need to tell that hospital bed

you didn't need it. Today you dress
in front of the same fireplace we huddled around

after snowy days, the warmth luring cats for naps.
The same fireplace you sucked embers from, imploding

the Red Devil®. Today your legs bow,
thighs separate, muscles missing. Unashamed,

I stare at your body that birthed me, the one
that engulfs me, still.

HOW TO SURVIVE

Buy a gun, sleep with it
beside your bed

It will remind you to feel safe
that you want to be alive. Call

the recipient of your last anger:
apologize. Mean it.

Buy a cactus on clearance.
Fertilize it,

but don't care
too much if it won't respond.

Don't believe in love, rather
live like it's all you have left

in your back pocket, with a hole
put there from a cigarette

by the last person who walked out on you.
Finger paint the last dream you had

with primary colors
and add too much yellow

because it blends with everything.
Write a card to someone dead

because you should have done it
when they were alive.

Experiment

If you don't have anything nice to say, write it down.

My Father Tells Me I Am a Girl

Air hung thick with water,
feels like walking between clothes lines of freshly

hung laundry. The sun is a proud chest, a man, made burly.
My father, legs locked out, torso bent over, picking weeds.

His body glistens with sweat puddled at dimples
on lower back. We work like this in the garden, no shirts,

exposed to summer. He teaches me how to dislodge an overly ripe
tomato from its vine without bruising delicate skin.

He knows my small hands are careful, will take their
time with such a task. He uses his calloused hands to pluck

prickly cucumbers, knows his blisters and layers of work hands
can endure the occasional sting. We garden because he knows how,

because he comes from a long line of sharecroppers, of work
on land that will never be theirs. We garden because it costs little

and (potentially), reaps food. It took me years to understand that last part.
One afternoon he peels his shirt, hangs it on the shovel's handle

I do the same. I always do the same. I learned to skip
river rocks this way, learned to blow my nose, holding one nostril

down with a thumb this way. *Put your shirt back on.* These words hang
like dry, starched jeans on our clothesline. I meet his eyes with mine,

don't understand. When you grow up emulating someone
you don't know how to question them. It works well for them,

it mostly, works for you. *It's hot,* I offer. *You are going to school next month.*
When it gets hot at recess you can't just take off your shirt. You are a girl.

I glared at his form: the tautness of skin to shoulders, his chest
hair damp, droplets collecting, outweighed by gravity.

Being a girl meant wearing more clothes, meant
I was a girl because of the potential of my body. I am a girl

because of what others might assume. For years
I assume my hands aren't meant for gardening,

were one day made wrong for planting, for picking. Did you know
your body is never safe? Did you know your parents are taught

to tell you how to wear your skin? I know now he said it with
tenderness masquerading as toughness, I know

these things are not mine and so I can move on.

89%

You've been alive for two years
and one month. Your oncologist said,

two or three years. You don't know he told me that.
I asked when you were in the bathroom

urinating morphine and fluids. He said,
Colleen has responded well to treatments,

and I conceptualize a machine: it sucks cancer
from your bones, licks the lesions from your abdomen.

It absorbs the splitting nail beds from your toes,
and fingers. It seals the cuts, skin breaking too soon.

This machine is a semi-automatic
shooter of pain management

which is why the bullets
are stored 100 at a time in the handle.

The double row of teeth keep
the oxycodone tablets sleek so swallowing

is effortless, no esophageal scratches
for the next year. The finger grooves

are for your hand only so you can control what you take,
leave, refuse, give, when to stop.

WET

The first time I remember being
at the ocean I submerged my whole head
and my father jerked me from the wave
cleared my eyes with his thumbs
and yelled *Never do that again!*
tears streaking through sunscreen
down his quivering cheeks.

When armpits get wet you need
to slather deodorant to mitigate the mess
our reproductive health teacher announced.
Maybe I was embarrassed she had to say that
or maybe I was already wearing deodorant
but likely I was too busy eyeing a girl
who's lips glistened because she licked
them every time she was praised for a right answer.

My mouth salivates after biting into
a lemon wedge and I know
there's no thirst quenching
but there is swallowing
and I run my tongue across the
rind, part sections, suck harder,
press pulp to gums and chew.

RECITATION

You have cancer
the word reborn in my mouth
like poems can be prayers
hear it, say it.

The word reborn in my mouth
living in your intestines
hear it, say it:
I wish you didn't have to write that poem

living in your intestines
we hear the gurgle
I wish you didn't have to write that poem
about me, for me.

We hear the gurgle
like poems can be prayers
about me, for me.
You (still) have cancer.

Variations of Silence

Down a highway, I live (not with you),
this May evening
lightly humid, grassy breezes, quiet, I imagine you in sleep,
the purr, pronounced lumps of life tucked around you
the littered books on your nightstand, book-marked pages, poems
read and unread, patient verses
or maybe you lay awake, supine
desperate for sleep but watch the slants of light peak
through your door, night gets to hold you,
wrap its presence to your skin.
This road between us is short enough to travel,
vast enough to keep us apart:
I hear your subtle gasps tonight, know your eyes
aroused glance up, the streetlight outlining
your welcoming, warm lips
where language and unlanguage speak together.

*Tent camping, dancing on bars and skinny dipping are always fun,
but do it all when you're young: the recovery is hell when you're old.*

Cannonball

I. Cannonballing

was how I met her: mess of salt-surfer strands,
sunshine sprigs flying,
a wave grin, bounce back
to grass slivers, to bleak ground.

I imagine her years later, cannonball body rolling
across Caribbean cliffs, tromping on trails,
laughter bellowing, palm trees echoing the boom.

Did you want to cannonball from that cliff?
(You know the one) The one everyone else
could merely rope swing from?
What if I were swimming by?
What if I were drowning?

II. Technique

If you tuck hard & clasp arms around
shins, hold opposite leg with hand

& push your head toward your knees
your ass will splat perfectly on the surface.

Your ass, splatting the surface.

The surface being splat by your ass.

As asses splat yours would surpass the splats before.

I am watching your ass to see the splat.

Splattering water splashes from your ass.

There are droplets on my toes from your ass.

This is what a hard tuck gets you.

Radiation

Lay still
so we can trace the line
mark the X
target the X
penetrate your bladder and bowels
radiate you through the X
strike lower than spinal cord
blast above coccyx.
Don't move.
We need to bulls' eye the X
blastocyst the tumor nestled, egg unhatched.
Lay still
so the finale is quiet
don't breathe
don't swallow.

WHEN YOUR BODY IS QUEER

you don't get to announce, I am non-normative.
If your gait is tightrope tethered to acceptability
I dare you to claim: I don't aspire to be palatable
so others can chew
slowly and quietly.

I confess: I let respectability politics
slather me in shame, my frame
walked sidewalks confident I wasn't "too queer"

and how did that save me?
I'm a temple of turmoil, boiling point
any degrees, and still
when eyes rest over me, tell me
I'm "beautiful"
translate "femme enough"
transcribe "diet dyke"
tattoo "traitor"
I smile.

So many souls sleep because
I know how to sit: legs crossed
at ankles, eyes lined under lubricated lashes.

So many hands shake mine
because I won't squeeze
too hard

won't stare down
the legitimacy of male bodies
lacking masculinity
that never earned
but rather assumed
or worse selfishly stolen.

I'm saying passing is nothing more
than a pivot stance and I thought
I was going for a lay-up
but really I've been in the lane
five seconds.

At Gender Reveals
I imagine taking my own cake to cut:
unveil rainbow-baked batter
divided by confectioner's frosting,
and I'd chew, lick my lips,
suck fork prongs.
I don't like remembering what norms

have done to my body.

When I do, can't claim
I don't grin.

Folx should
send shame cards
to me
call it Valentine's.

My calloused hands
should next time
grip girl's,
kiss man's.

Recovery

Did you taste metal? Is under your tongue still dry, her nurse asks. My mother's body is a wooded holler, a thicket being bulldozed, a rainforest being outsourced. Her tumors make diamonds in bone's marrow, the pressure of cancer cells punching out, trying to escape, burst her marrow, gems coast through bloodstreams. I call Vectibix® the pan, sifting cancer cells, I mean diamonds, salvaged put on sale, making Mom marketable. The Camptosar®, her compass, hair thins, skin breaks, pores widen as skin flakes in her hands. We are told side effects equate to potency.

If anyone asks where you're from tell them nowhere they've been:
it will keep them wondering and you safe.

FERTILE

Limbs lay with veins pulsing as mountains: your skin becomes valleys. Your limbs don't sway anymore on dance floors. Come morning I massage coconut oil and lavender into your forested arms, watering the terrain. There are no scars on your skin, I know, I've traced every inch. Your body wasn't built to last, wasn't fabricated for invading tumors, for lymph nodes abandoning you. Often you ask me to leave for travel or work. I can't go just yet, but you know this: we are intertwined, honeysuckles vining a farm fence.

Your dad's family is special, so treat them as such: special people who should be caged, studied and documented but never set free.

The Study

Someone wants to study your body
(not the way I study bodies)

in a way that dissects your tissues,
syringes your blood and slides

cells under microscopes. They want to watch
your cancer stem cells grow: *In addition*

to the treatment described in this consent form,
the study sponsor would like to store blood

and tumor tissue samples for future
scientific research studies. Where will you

be stored? May I come, pull the vile labeled
"Colleen Margaret Ouellette Cooper, 9/19/1952"

from its cabinet when specimens are all that remain,
when I need you to tell me how to fold

a fitted sheet or the amount of time one
should work with pastry dough?

ANALYSIS & CONCLUSIONS

FOR VISION'S SAKE

My father's first memory of his mother
is in a cotton patch: her body bent
hustling down a row, plucking future t-shirts,
he sat on a sheet spread
where burlap bags bulged with boll until dumped.

When your first memory of your mother
is her walking away
while you can only crawl
you earn a rambling heart.
Also, you earn eyes
that strain to see people
as they distance into nothingness.

Today my father said:
*In the end some people find Jesus and some people
find their family.* I wanted to ask: what if one isn't looking
for either?

I wanted to tell him Jesus drew lines in the sand too
and some family isn't worth finding. I wanted
to whisper: *no one is walking out of
your cataracts sight today.*

Some people aren't meant to have children, and some are smart enough to know that.

Undoing Dollhood

On Michigan Avenue I walk
past the American Girl Doll Store

& flinch against skyscraping statures
with gold lettering. As a child I wanted

not to own Samantha but to be her. Her hair
straight yet curled under (only at the ends)

her eyes brown, but not too brown,
those golden flecks of light prevented

dullness of too dark brown, like mine.
Her skin cream, not olive, like mine,

her hands soft, manicured, not grasping
a baseball bat or smashed in a catcher's

mitt or sweating in gloves ready
to fast pitch a snowball against a telephone pole.

Regifting is a gift.

Again, Again

What I took to be a bookshelf, half vacant
vertical lines, jutting and cutting space
turned out to be a floating staircase
spiraled like a deck of cards, mid-shuffle.
What I wanted to be tea steeping at dawn
was really candle flame of wick burning
into glass.
It was my wanting coercing me,
begging me to see what
couldn't be
what never was – my wanting
making wine corks into crayons
shifting curtains into scarves
and it was this wanting
that controlled me: what I imagined
to be a poem in my pocket
was really soiled tissues,
and when I thought I heard
How many times can you really start?
I responded, *again, again*
but there was no voice.
I want to say *we are being honest*
which is to announce: we are
making silence in a library.
But here I am: back to wanting books on shelves.
If I let air slip slowly through pursed lips I can hear
the footsteps ascending stairs:
a whisper from sole
of foot to step,
and I can see a splinter erect
in the corner, near spindling wood.
I place left hand to railing,
guide fingers to grip, make a fist around
the iron cylindrical metal
I climb, call your name
find you there, sleeping
in a bed
I wish I had never known
without you.

I Called My Mother

After viewing Laura Aguilar's photography

I called my mother to say I love you
        and art came rolling out. I couldn't not
                tell her of the bodies in black and white
                        who were really brown, that fell
                                like tired trees on canvas making caverns.

I called my mother to say I love you
        and she said my dad had been
                at the elementary school for their grandson's
                        father-son breakfast. She said he is glad to go,
                                said he's sad he has to be father and grandfather.

I called my mother to say I love you
        and I was carrying a tray of coffees
                to serve my friends, wanted to wake
                        and nourish them, wanted my body to be of use.

Flu Season

She stayed home every day,
  didn't want to risk contamination
    be validated: immune system too run down.

At least that's what we told people:
  declined parties & dinner invites,
    bowed graciously, out of school plays.

Really, we were trying to preserve her,
  brine her in Epsom salt baths, keep her
    hydrated in essential oils and salves.

We were slowing her down. We were asking time to forget us.

DON'T TELL ME YOU LOVE ME

Don't tell me you love me after we have sex
because I love lots of things after an orgasm,
my skin is brighter, lips saltier:
Joy can be measured
in the distance between two blissed bodies
but that is not love, that is gratitude.

Don't say it in my parent's home
because one day it will be sold
and I will be old, and we don't know
the first thing about love in the presence
of two people: waving off time
with a white flag.

Don't tell me you love me
because I will say it back.

Don't tell me you love me
because when I say it back you will believe me.
My throat is a loose cannon in a civil war reenactment
and dear, you should not be a battleground.

Don't tell me you love me
because I will say it back
like I've said it before: I have said it
over twenty times and I've only meant it twice
and the time I meant it most
I felt my brain bash itself into skull
and heart stop beating
because it needed a beat down instead.

So, don't say it, say something else:
I love the way you hold me.
I love how funny you are when you're uncomfortable.
I love when your hands talk for your mouth
because I don't know which to watch.
Say something like that and after awhile
I'll know you love me but the moment you say it
I'm an earthquake waiting to split surface,
pull you in. And let me say:
I never want to be someone's natural disaster.

Don't tell me you love me
because these words are popcorn
and that's just something to stick in my teeth,
an annoyance to toothpick out.
These words are so common
they are a currency I have accepted every time:

empty my pockets, sew them closed.
I'll let you, knowing I'll have nowhere
to shield my hands when nervous or cold
because you are a seamstress and I
want a new exchange rate valued in thread colors.

But if you've found a way around my lines,
then say it on a day that is ordinary:
walk to work, drink stale coffee, say it after a lunch
of iceberg salad with packeted ranch dressing
and three-day croutons, say it after
you've called your mom just to hear her voice.

Say it on that day when you could have said anything.
Say it but keep your mouth closed.
Open your eyes.
Don't say my name.
Remember yours.

Paddle in Your Wake

If I may say: there are raindrops on my lips
I need to roll below your belly.
There's a blanket on my chest
I still call grandma.
My soul is a stillness in which I've crammed so many fears
I hear whimpers each time I wear earbuds.

Wrap your arm through mine
and say *I have you*
even if you can't mean it
because maybe I need
to hear it. And maybe, just maybe
you need
to let it go.

Hold me until my arms become ivy
curling around your waist,
until my legs knot, cinch closed, pelvic bones
rooted in your inner thighs.
For any other woman I'd smile
but you would never let me succumb to blushing
against a sunny afternoon.
For you
I'd sit
face to face.

We were talking of rivers and ripples
when you announced, *I can swim faster than anyone.*

I acknowledged, *I'll paddle in your wake.*
So, my knotted body cleaves
to your words. On banks I skip rocks
faster, farther away from driftwood
and beaver dams.
You can find momentum in places
you can't find hope.
So, when you say you miss me
I want to believe I make you hungry.
My legs want you to shiver, want you
to call them back, rest me
in your lap.

CONTRAPUNTAL OF EMBODIMENT

"Suppose that truth is a woman – and why not?" -Nietzsche, Preface to *Beyond Good and Evil*

You spent the morning bouldering   We spent the night gripping anything
       clamping edges, fingers bound, knotted,
palms (now hardened)   tell me of your route, I'll tell you
       the look of your brow is fatigued but pleased,
hands hugging each crevice,
feet cradled in nooks,
       arms straining to grasp one last hold,
look up, close eyes.   my back, now half-mooned indentions.
       You left finger-spot-bruises,
       I found them days later   in a mirror meant for make-up & tooth-
       brushing.

Relax hands
exasperated gasp, your body releases.
You let go, rest under
a shadow shrouds
       grasp anything
       in that kind of light, that kind of dark.

Handscape

Her hands were sheer fabric
sliding over hip bones, down thighs.
They were sharpened garden shears
slicing bushes needing pruning
leaving yard art.
There are things we must know
and things we can't.

I choose to love   this time   for once
with all my intelligence
is inked on my right shoulder. It's permanence
left me bleeding upon tattooing, speechless upon reading

because this hunger is an oak tree,
fingers are taproot-thirsty toward water
that is her. I wonder if Tee Corrine would
document us, title the exhibit
"Handscape" or if she would only want
to know how our thighs wrapped
arms vined across torsos, hands escaping, camera clicking

as legs straddled, hands splayed across shoulders,
I squeeze my palms,
mouth open to diaphragm
any air. My lungs will never forget

this expansion: breath straining to pace
this ride. And I knew it couldn't last forever
but I also believe in miracles: In utero we divide
millions of times, each an opportunity for failure
and yet somehow we emerge screaming,
breaking frail finish line tape
we could never see.

And I've never been one to stand still
but every rainbow has an arc
and every arc has a decent
that is fading against the atmosphere
and I'm pausing as I feel you sink
into sheets your body slowing, tensing,
your breath arcing
thanking your bones.

RESULTS

Flying, a Question

Ask me about the time I misfired,
       shot cold ground: one foot in front of my boot

instead of tin can on tree stump.
       It felt like gratitude, sound of low thud,

like your heart dropping to earth
       knowing it won't survive a place like this.

Ask me how I know what can survive.
       I'll answer you: birds. Their furcula is how.

Ask me what a furcula is. It's what you call
       a wishbone, a fusion of matter, a reckoning from the ground.

Ask me if I've ever held one end
       of the furcula and snapped it for luck.

Ask me what it felt like to break
       something's only chance to leave.

I'll tell you even birds can't outrun bullets.

In the Kitchen with my Father

You have always cleaned the cookie sheets
with too much soap: in the sink you spin,
scrub, flip and rinse.

You say: *I've got this, go sit with your mom.*

I say: *she's in the bathroom.*

You say: *how do you know?*

I say: *I hear her toothbrush sounds.*

How Masculinity Isn't Medicine

I want to tell my father his masculinity will
not save him from this.

Say: Dad, your masculinity will fail you.
See how I put masculinity and failure

in the same sentence? Now, I'll put it on
the same line: masculinity will fail you.

And now side by side:
masculinity fails.

Now, I'll put it on.

YOU ARE TRYING

to remember how
it happened　　　　　You are trying to
remember these events in a sensible
order　　　　　Your father was sleep deprived
so he wasn't thinking
He had been trying to rest
at least you remember him lying in bed
chest rising, breath released over curled torso hair
He was too asleep
You were befuddled by the sleep
since his wife was screaming　　　　　next to him
You recall he was still snoring when your feet hit
the landing of the stairs　　　　　and you heard
a thud and a new kind of breath
a gasping breath　　　　　His wife was now
on the floor　　　　　but she was still breathing
You think there was confusion
she shook with a chill being uncovered
being now exposed　　　　　she was limp
In darkness you moved toward her
maybe sat her up, wrapped her arms over your neck
likely placed hands under her arms, hoisted her up onto the bed
You probably kissed her as you did this, whispered kindness
into her ears　　　　　She likely couldn't hear you
He, your father, is still sleeping next to her　　　　　You don't want to blame him
You are scared in a home with your mother days from dying,
your father just over-medicated on morphine　　　　　You want night to end
so a nurse will come and tell you everything is as it should be
There was blood on her leg, your mother's　　　　　You searched her body for origin
and found a toenail　　　　　Snagged on the sheets, it caught when she fell
from the bed
You spend the next five minutes cutting all her toenails
then fingernails, just in case　　　　　She lets you
she doesn't know who you are, you think
You don't go back to bed　　　　　you sit on the sofa
you listen to their breathing sounds:
his are deep-throaty, they are heavy chest rises and lungs expanding
hers are upper-back-of-the-throat choking-gurgling-of-lungs
You start referring to yourself as "witness"
You remind yourself you are also still their daughter.

Re-gifting is a gift.

PANTOUM FOR DEPARTING

If you're still living, consider:
who will autograph your tombstone?
What human will wait 'til you're lowered
and chisel you a love letter in granite?

Who will autograph your tombstone
she asked me lying in her death bed.
Then, chiseled letters of love with granite teeth
and bit her lips, chewed cheeks,

she asked me, lying in her death bed
if I *had a poem that rhymed*
and bit her lips, chewed tattered cheeks.
She said she needed something to focus on.

If you had a poem that rhymed
I'd remain respectfully fascinated,
she said. We needed something to focus on,
needed syncopated sounds.

I'd remain respectfully fascinated
on the rhythm and repetition
of our need for syncopated sounds.
She knows she can't, do this alone.

On rhythm and repetition
what human will wait 'til you're lowered?
She knows she can't do this, alone.
If you're still living, consider.

In the Mourning

No one came. For twenty-four hours
my father and I sat in the home he built

her thirty years ago, we listened to the echoes of her body:
acoustics agonized of gurgle breaths, the reverberation

from bricks to cedar beams to ceiling.
In the mourning I am told she is no longer

suffering. I am told she is in a better place. I am told
things that no one knows to be true. In the mourning, I am told things to comfort

the one telling me things. I am told no one came
at the end because they didn't want to remember her like that:

dying, skin stretched over cheekbones, eyes open,
mouth unable to speak, in a diaper, fluid moving toward lungs.

Last Sacraments

I figured I should be there / knew I should talk to you / murmur things like: *it's time to say good-bye* / *I will be okay without you* / You know, lies like that / I read something to you / poems I'd written / over fifty pages of verse as you heaved hard / gurgled / released inaudible yelps / I cleaned your body / wipes and warm washcloths over sun-splotched skin, soothed lotion into vascular arms / clipped unpainted toenails / cupped my hands toward your mouth as you opened wide / one last time: the cancer leaking out like an exorcism gone right / you hurled the cancer contents of your stomach / the purple-black liquid that choked you / for days.

If you drink three cups of yerba mate tea before hitting the cocktails, you're always better off.

Our First Dance was to a Resistance Song

"What's unique about language is that creatures who develop it are highly vulnerable to being eaten." – Temple Grandin, *Animals in Translation: Using the Mysteries of Autism to Decode Animal Behavior*

In college I chose girlfriends based on their dancing skills.
You say this frying bacon. It sizzles. I snicker.

With candor you confess,
I thought, if we were compatible on the dance floor

we would be sexually compatible too.
I adore that young dyke in you, the one

who fashioned standards on sliding scales,
who kept quiet to keep alive, the one

who avoided speaking to me until
I asked for math tutoring.

Back then you wore flannel button-downs.
Did you know I remember that of you?

If you ever talk to that girl, the one
who wouldn't look at me, tell her

There ain't no easy way out.
Tell her at a salty bar

during an afternoon storm, you leaned
into me and I took your hand

to dance across salt-speckled planks.
Tell her *But I'll stand my ground*

And I won't back down.

Shots (& Other Things She Taught Me)

She once outdrank the church choir director,
my elementary art teacher, her cosmetologist, me, my father

and a man twice her body weight.
She shamed us in her home with a tequila shot glass

and no salt. My mother was not liver strong
but bar stool smart: tossing tequila shots

over her shoulder in lieu of down her throat.
She told me once, *thrills instigate desire.*

I wish I wanted something as bad as my mother wanted me.
She wanted no children, she said, until one day her hunger turned

to appetite turned to starved for a baby.
That's what she said until one day she said,

I never wanted children I always wanted you.
And, I didn't understand that at the time

and I still can't fathom wanting anyone that way
but I do know she never lied.

You have so much to offer but don't show all your cards at once: the rules of dating and gambling are interchangeable.

COLLARBONE

I get night sweats when it's a quarter moon,
hungry waking from naps.
I inhale eucalyptus to ease my body.

My body is all mine
if I can essential oil it sweetly
to relaxation.

You won't know me if I never speak.
You are no linguist.

I swear my lips are somewhere
tasting the skin of a woman
who loved me best before she knew
I can put all my hurt in a backpack
and run as fast with it as without it.

When my mother died I watched the pulse
stop in her collarbone and swore
I'd never gnaw a baby back rib again.
To be truthful I couldn't eat meat for months.

I never hungered to be vegetarian
but watching a body succumb to death complicated
notions of nourishment.

Next spring I'll plant a garden to sustain me
for summer. I promise.

I'm Going to Tell You What She Tastes Like

Salty. A little dry. She's not quite crunchy
though somewhat grainy. She is soft,
melts on the tongue
dissolves really.

He licks his finger
presses it to ashes
that was her body
that was her flesh
that is her now
that I watched die
whose last breath
was a choke of air
clean mountain air.

How does one choke
on clean mountain air?

His index finger, iced with ashes,
disappears in his mouth.

He swallows: *she tastes like home.*

Putting me in a nursing home will only ensure your life to forever be haunted by a post-menopausal ghost.

[i walk with your hand in mine (i walk with you]

AFTER E.E. CUMMINGS

[i walk with your hand in mine (i walk with you]
r hand in mine)i am always with it(nowhere
i go are you absent, my girl; and what thoughts
are mine are for you, my dream)
                       i resolve
no life(for you make me feel alive, touch life)I have
a plan(for the compass you are, my direction)
and you are what due north has always been
and where south will always sleep

here is the cavernous truth everyone knows
(here is the tentacle of the octopus and the pad of the paw
and the rain of a cloud on a petal called sunflower; that thrives
faster than any stalk can fathom or neck can crane)
and here is the magic that separates protons and electrons

[i walk with your hand in mine (i walk with you]

Making bets with me is a bad idea—me losing means you losing.

Universal

If you use only the periodic table
one can argue the moon and earth
are identical twins.

It's true: they share
the same isotopes.
To be fair though, I prefer
earthy things:
wet dirt over worn
hiking boots, hands
calloused from
wooden shovel
handles, tan lines
splitting across scapulas.

Put it another way:
the shine of
shin skin when shaving,
rain-slick
highways evaporating
to heat
and the hum of
nothingness
(though that may
be procured
on the moon too)
is where I want to live.

If you think too much
or not enough
you can convince
yourself of anything
or of everything.

HANDS & MOUTH

I strike a match / to burn
sage / bundles smoke circles
/ in every room / of my silent
home / I do / this often / I do
it infrequently enough / to
forget / to do it / more often
/ often I'm too busy smack-
ing / I mean striking gum
between teeth / When I was
fourteen I got braces / for my
imperfect smile / for dental
health / for other reasons
too / my parents couldn't
afford them / but wanted
my mouth / to smile proud
/ One Christmas / I drank
too much tequila / and said
something like Mom / this
mouth has afforded / many
a woman / many a / pleasure
/ she maybe said / your
tequila tongue lives behind
/ white / straight teeth / in a
queer mouth / your face is
striking / either way though
/ I strike a match / burn sage
/ hold it to my face / under
my nostrils / wave it over /
my head / past my shoulders
/ open a bottle / brace for
quivering lips / let her ashes
soar / over Stoney Lake /
they never strike water / but
land / over / quiet ripples.

Centered

Once, I read the heart pumps 2,000 gallons of blood
every day. My mother always had a gallon of milk

in the fridge: she would pour it in thick mason jars
at dinner, over ice. *Milk should be consumed perfectly chilled,*

she would say. Wouldn't drink it any other way,
made me drink two glasses daily as I refused

to be breast fed for the first month of life.
Newborn babies have the fastest heart rate

the pediatrician told my mother. She heard
there's an organ tied to hummingbird wings

in your daughter's thoracic. The tie-dye t-shirt
I wore until someone peeled it from me

smelled of vinegar and indigo: rings punching
across cotton fabric. In fifth grade I learned

an adult heart is the size of a fist and situated
in the middle of one's chest. That felt fitting to remember

when my mom died. Not from heart cancer
which is rare since heart cells stop dividing:

less room for error, for mutation. Either way the heart
still beats 115,000 times a day. When mom's stopped,

mine wanted to sync to hers the way
a horse's heart can mirror a human's. *I don't like*

all these feelings I finally acknowledge to my doctor.
Your heart can beat outside your chest, they insisted.

I responded, *then take it out.*

DUBLIN, WITHOUT YOU

For Catherine

In a city you adore
on an island I passenger through
you call to remind me: find the bookstore
then the whiskey bar.
Your hungry words suspend time
& I imagine us as travel companions:
we walk, stroll
through cobblestoned curves, bottle caps
pressed between mud, the way anything can find space
with enough force.
& what we hear
from guitar strums and drumming hands
is the cacophony of a city
that welcomes us.
& what we know is we must
stay, must hold the sunshine
in our bellies, the rain clouds
in our mouths.
We become an open field.
Grass blading ankles, wind across your flushed
and dimpled cheeks, words spill from my mouth,
The most important thing I've ever built in my life
is your trust.

ELEGY TO THOSE I THOUGHT WRONG FOR STAYING IN THE CLOSET

I want to write a love poem to all those people
I thought needed to come out:

say to them, you were out, in ways illegible to me.
I thought coming out was emancipation,

was proud occupancy. What I couldn't read were gestures:
nights she slept in my twin bed, our bodies sharing heat

but never skin and afternoons we lounged on docks,
feet submerged in lake water too cold. What I couldn't hear

was silence: we were making language from rooms
where words weren't the metric. What I couldn't believe in

was my own forgiveness.
Last night I showed her my heart.

It pumped, thudded, thrashed. It acted contained, disgruntled.
I had never seen it, my heart that is. Though I was sure

I had one. It was even in the right spot, slightly left
of center. To look at the heart she had to press

a lubricated ultrasound wand near my sternum.
She had to find my heart. *That's your mitral valve,*

your left and right ventricle, and that's your inferior vena cava,
her finger pointing to iPad's screen.

& I said, it looks like a clenched fist.
& she offered, it's a muscle.

& I said, it isn't as strong as it looks.
& she announced, there's four valves, all flapping.

& I said, that heart has wronged the wrong people
& she promised, the valves are still flapping.

THE THRASHING

Still I tread water anytime I try
to float. It's the stillness I can't rest in.

The summer you taught me to swim
an instructor said *hold your child*

we're going to dunk them on three.
I hovered supine above your arms

& into your eclipsed face whispered
promise you won't dunk me ok?,

& you nodded & I went back
to watching clouds float & I was trying

to show you I was good
at being still when water rushed

through my nostrils. I thrashed to surface,
sputtering, coughing. You never apologized.

My recollection, now confused if you
ever agreed to not submerge me, the pull

of my body underwater, the chlorinated gulps,
blare of my own yelps as I found my way

back to air, back to your sunlit
body. That day

I thought you wanted me to feel
what dying would be like.

Today I know I had to learn
how not to drown.

ACKNOWLEDGMENTS

"89%" *Pink Panther Review*, March 2019

"A Conversation with my Mother" *Cahaba Literary Review*, April 2015

"Body Cartographer" Wolfpack Press, *Winter Solstice*, December 21, 2018

"Cannonball" *Room*, January 2020

"Centered" *Iron Horse Literary Review*, Spring 2020 & *Ice on a Hot Stove*, May 2021

"Dreaming of the Dead" *Pink Panther Review*, March 2019

"Drafting" *Pilgrimage*, March 2019

"Flu Season" *Pioneertown*, April 2020

"Fireplace" *Quiet Storm*, Fall 2018

"Grandma's House" *Shot Glass Journal*, June 2014

"Hands & Mouth" *Lunch*, October 2019 & *Ice on a Hot Stove*, May 2021

"Hiking With an Erasure Heart" *Ice on a Hot Stove*, May 2021

"How Masculinity Isn't Medicine" *Pioneertown,* April 2020

"Indignant" *Quiet Storm*, Fall 2018

"I Wanna Be A Drag Queen" *Sling Magazine*, February 15 2015

"My Mother Dreams of the Dead" *Pink Panther Review*, March 2019

"My Mother as Lymph Nodes" & "Liver Lesions" *Melancholy Hyperbole* 2014

"Paddle in Your Wake" *Pink Panther Review*, September 2018

"Pantoum for Departing" *Adanna Literary Journal*, October 2019 & *Ice on a Hot Stove*, May 2021

"Performing Basic Instinct" *Adanna Literary Journal*, October 2019

"Predisposed" *Helen Literary Magazine*, June 2017 & *Manticore: Hybrid Writing from Hybrid Identities*, May 2019

"Recitation" *Quiet Storm,* Fall 2018

"Testament" *Pink Panther Review*, March 2019

"The Study" *Forage Poetry: Poetry of Politics*, November 2016

"Thursday Nights at The Islander" *Relentless: Wild Age Press*, June 2015

"Variations of Silence" *Vitamin Zzz: RESET BUTTON*, Spring 2018